How to Love Yourself

Yourself

A guide to building your self-esteem when you don't know where to start

LAKEYSHA-MARIE GREEN

"Attaining inner peace isn't about letting someone else read your lines; it's about embracing your character and giving the performance of a lifetime. Never be afraid to express your inner thoughts, never be afraid to dance to a different beat because when you shine with self-acceptance, *you light up the world*."

-Lakeysha-Marie Green, Author

Table of Contents

INTRODUCTION

You've heard it a thousand times.

It's becoming more and more unpopular to love yourself. Television, marketing, popularity contests, unrealistic expectations and advertising have led you to think that no matter what you do, you won't be worthy until you buy this next product, or act like this other person, or look like the hottest movie star. That may be all fine and well if it weren't for the fact that this *isn't true*.

How many rich and famous people do you know of who have serious issues? Even some of those that are portrayed as the most successful still can't seem to find a sense of self-love and self-worth.

It's important to always strive to improve your life, but there is no magic pill or facial cream that's going to do it. Happiness doesn't come from what you buy, where you shop, what you wear or even by what other people think of you. *Real* happiness comes from within.

There is such a large market for unhappy people because there are so many people who don't know how to be happy. It is my hope that within these pages, you can find some insight and some useful tips to help you on your own path toward discovering personal happiness.

Just like everything else, this book isn't a magic wand. The most important things in life require effort, and the effort involved in this proposition isn't a small one, but it's well worth it... and you just might be surprised at how much simpler it is than living a life without self-love.

A couple of articles struck me recently, and I will reference them periodically throughout these pages. The original articles can be found:

http://www.huffingtonpost.com/margaret-paul-phd/love-yourself_b_4218211.html
Authored by Margaret Paul, Ph.D.

and

http://www.psychologytoday.com/blog/finding-love/201105/how-love-yourself-first
Authored by Ken Page, LCSW

I encourage you to read these articles yourself, as they have within them some amazing insights into the importance of self-love and things that you can do *that work*.

Along with reference to these materials, I will also share my own insight into the matter: what has worked for me and what has worked for others. Life is too short to spend it without loving yourself. Here's hoping that this humble text can be of help to you on your path through life.

CHAPTER 1: TRUSTING YOURSELF

The obvious reasons to love yourself need not be mentioned too in depth here, we all know that a lack of self-love can lead to low self-esteem, depression, anxiety and a slew of other maladies both physical and mental. But there is more.

When you don't love yourself, you are not truly free. If you don't trust in yourself, you have a tendency to put a great deal of trust into other people.

The problem with this is that, just like us, these other people are not perfect. Whether these people lead us in the wrong direction intentionally or simply due to their inability (and the utter impossibility) of another person *really* knowing what is best for each of us in every situation, the fact is that not loving ourselves enough to trust ourselves, our beliefs and our values can often be bowled over by the very people that we hold in high regard.

This is in no way meant to suggest that we can't or shouldn't trust other people. Trust is a crucial part of any healthy relationship. Rather, that without loving ourselves enough to trust ourselves first, we are certain to go down many roads that we don't want to go down.

Take a moment to think about a person that you know personally and trust implicitly (other than yourself.) What are the characteristics of this person that make it possible for you to feel confident in your trust in them? What sort of impact has this person had on your life?

Now, ask yourself this one question: Is this person perfect?

Even were the answer to this question to be yes, that would only mean that this person would be perfect in their own lives.

From the people that we trust, we can learn a lot about ourselves. The things that we admire in these people are things that we strive to have in our own lives. Whether it's integrity, honesty, courage, strength, sensitivity, etc., these are things that we value.

What can you do in your own life to gain or enhance these qualities within yourself, and in your own way? What works for one person doesn't always work in someone else, but the underlying motivation behind these things: the will to be honest; the will to be strong, are in themselves motivation toward that end.

Nobody should be blindly followed, but at the same time, there is something that we can learn from everyone. Even if someone is simply an example of what not to do, they can be learned from. Those who inspire us deserve our appreciation, and the *courtesy* to not be thought of as perfect. That is a weight that nobody can shoulder for very long.

When we are young, we begin to learn "our role." This concept is a social construct that simplifies our society into different subsets of people based on birth, wealth, demeanor, aptitude, etc. ad nauseam. In English? It's a way of telling a rectangular peg that it's a square because it has four sides. The problem is, it doesn't fit.

I humbly submit that it's not the metaphorical peg (the individual) that needs to change its shape, but the board (societal perspective) that needs to work to accommodate the individuality of its pieces (people.) There are, of course, laws which are necessary to maintaining peace, however, these often aren't the biggest takeaway that we have from learning our "role."

When we are children, we have a much better idea of who we are than we often do as adults. Yes, there is much that we don't know about the world, society, etc., but there is something that most children are unquestionably aware of: how they feel.

Take a moment and think about a child that you know. Let's be honest. They're weird.

They make up crazy stories with such vehemence that you'd almost believe them. They play games with inanimate objects, and have a blast doing it. They talk to themselves, some even make up their own languages. In an adult, we'd often consider any one of these a symptom of a mental disorder, but in children, it's absolutely normal. More than that, playing pretend and other things that kids do, are crucial to their development.

Kids aren't necessarily the most honest people in the world to other people, but they are incredibly honest with themselves. The funny thing is, as adults we find this difficult to achieve, but children do it without even thinking about it.

Some societal norms are there for our protection, and we can't always do everything that we want to do. If someone makes us angry in traffic, we may have glorious visions of knocking some sense into them, but this is rightly illegal. If everyone who got annoyed in traffic took their anger out on the driver in front of them, we'd all have plenty of bruises and broken bones for it.

However, when it comes to our personality, our beliefs, our values, our likes, our dislikes and the type of people with whom we enjoy association, going with *you* is the best decision that you can make.

If expressing yourself (even to yourself) isn't hurting you or anyone else, then, whether you're a Trekkie, a health nut or a Michael Bolton fan, why not let yourself be yourself?

If you're afraid that your friends won't accept you for who you really are, you're doing a disservice to yourself and to them by remaining in the "friendship." Friends are the people who stand by us and hold us up when the rest of the world tells us that we're strange.

While we're on the subject, I'm going to let you in on a little secret... *Everybody is strange.*

I honestly haven't met a single person in my life that didn't have their quirks or eccentricities. Even the most well-adjusted people that we know have, at one time or another, done or said something out of the ordinary. I'll go you one further. A person who is comfortable enough with him or herself to (forgive the colloquialism) "let their flag fly" is, in my opinion, more well-adjusted than those of us who spend our time trying to fit our rectangular pegs into square holes.

So, how does this have anything to do with self-love? The fact of the matter is that who we really are on the inside, the "me" that we know ourselves to be (whether anyone else does or not,) is important.

The more that we outwardly or inwardly try to reject the "inner me," the more that we injure ourselves and actually reinforce the idea that it's not okay to love ourselves.

Of course, if there are things about yourself which are unhealthy, they should be recognized for what they are, and work should be put forth to change those things; however, loving yourself who you *really* are, not just the façade that we put on for those around us is the true key to happiness, and it's from this deceptively simple act that all happiness springs.

CHAPTER 2: LEARNING HOW TO LISTEN

The word "listen" in this title is no idle term. There's a big difference between hearing and actually listening. In this chapter we'll focus on the only two groups that have any sort of importance in the world. You, and everyone else.

These groups are a lot more alike than you'd think. Sure, we're all pushed into being clichés so that others can say, "Oh, that's Cheryl the stock-broker," or "That's Jim, the weird guy down the street who waters his lawn fourteen hours a day." But apart from these vastly oversimplified and misleading attributes, there is a whole lot more to us, and the similarities always outweigh the differences.

We all want to be loved and to love someone else. We all want to be happy and successful, though our definitions may be different in regard to what that means to us individually. We all want to make our lives matter in some way, whether we want to be remembered as a good parent, a famous movie-star or the person who successfully watched every season of The Young and the Restless without leaving the couch once. (I shudder to think of the implications of that one.)

The fact is that there is you and there is the way that you fit into the world and the people whom make up your social circle.

Let's start at the beginning and the end: Listening to *you*.

People often have great insight, and that should not be ignored, however, what matters most is what *you* think about what you're doing.

Are you working in that job because it's something that you love doing, or because of the paycheck or social status? Are the people with whom you surround yourself in your life because they're uplifting and helpful, caring individuals, or because they're the more socially acceptable choice? Do you listen to the music that you do because it's popular, or because it speaks to your spirit in a way that can't be denied?

Part of trusting yourself is listening to *yourself*.

Human beings can endure all sorts of vile and horrendous things and, hopefully, what you do for a living doesn't fit into this category. But there is a difference between being able to tolerate what you do and loving what you do, and this extends to all areas of your life.

There are things that we all have to do in order to sustain our existence. We need to eat, drink, breathe, get some form of movement or exercise and be sheltered from the elements, at least enough to continue living, but how we do what we need to do and if/when we do what we want to do has a great impact on our happiness. We also have to have some sort of income to maintain our homes, pay our bills, and see to our other wants and needs, but again, it's not always in *what* we do, it's often in *how* we approach doing it.

In regard to work, sometimes we have to take a position that we don't like in order to get by. I know that I've had some crappy jobs that paid less than ten-percent of my worth, and I know that most of us are still there in one way or another. It's enjoying what you do that makes all of the difference in the world. Some of the happiest people in the world make pittance for a living, but they are happy to do it because they've finally listened to themselves and are doing something that they love.

Are you doing what you love? If so, great! If not, what steps would you have to take in order to get there? What sacrifices would you have to make in order to take these steps and, more importantly, what is the payoff if you do? Now, the most important question of all: What are you waiting for?

We can't all be movie-stars, but we can all find something that we love to do. It may take some time. We may have to take a lower paying position to get started, or go to college, or both, but answer me this question: is that really worse than doing something that you hate every day of your life for the foreseeable future?

The simple principle of listening to yourself is something which can guide you to a world that really reflects what you want out of life. The alternative is simply treading water, waiting for something to happen that never will while you whittle away your life working for a company that you don't believe in, only to come home to friends that you don't really like, surrounded by all sorts of possessions that you neither really want or really need. The choice is simple, but I won't say that it's easy.

The second part of this chapter is learning how to listen to others.

While it is important, first and foremost, to know your own feelings, beliefs and accept them for what they are, others can often give us perspective that we just don't have on our own.

How many times have you heard (or said) something to the effective, "_____ gave me the best advice, and it changed my life," or, "I should have listened?" Not everyone should be listened to every time, however, it's good to keep your ears open to those who may just have the answer to something that you've been looking for, whatever it is. When you trust yourself and listen to yourself first, you can learn to take suggestions from others when they're in line with your personal values.

When someone who is trustworthy gives you valuable advice, it's akin to working on an old ship. Sometimes we're too close to the water and the boat to see what's on the horizon. Therefore, we have trusted people as lookouts who can see whether we're heading toward a storm.

In the next chapter, we'll discuss more about surrounding yourself with uplifting people, but for now, let's take a moment to look a little bit more closely at how we can better listen to ourselves and others.

When you meet with your closest friends, how do you feel? Do you feel enlivened? Uplifted? Happy? Do you feel anxious? Uncomfortable? Just plain bored? Here's our first listening exercise: If you go over to a friend's house, and you find yourself wanting to leave as soon as you're through the door, what is this telling you?

Unless there's a particularly difficult, but healthy and necessary, situation taking place, chances are that this is a person for whom you don't feel true affinity. Whether they make you ill-at-ease, or they simply don't provide the fun or closeness that you're looking for in a friendship, then what are you really gaining by subjecting yourself to the relationship?

Family's a bit different, as we all know, but at the same time, if relations with one or more family members have degenerated to the point where you don't feel safe or valued while you're in their presence, then maybe it's time to let this person/these people know what the issue is and that you need to remove yourself until it changes.

Sometimes we need to take a difficult line in order to be true to ourselves, but the more we listen to our true nature, the happier that we will be and the less garbage we'll be willing to put up with from hurtful people.

CHAPTER 3: FRIENDS?

The people with whom we surround ourselves have an immense impact on who we are and how we feel about ourselves. Sometimes we're friends with a person because they were from the same neighborhood, or sometimes it's just convenient. More often than we may like to think, many times we start a friendship because the person appears to be someone that we could admire, but when the friendship solidifies, the person removes the mask to reveal the monster within.

The last sentence there may sound a bit dramatic, but I don't think that it's too far off in a lot of cases. Often times we make friends who then demand us to do things with which we are uncomfortable, or are simply out of our nature.

People like this prey on the kindness of others and the obligation that they'll be sure to remind you comes with friendship.

This is actually a function of the psychology related to public relations: If we do a favor for another person, they're more likely to do a favor for us, even if our favor is a lot bigger than the one that we performed in the first place. There are various terms for people like this, but one that I think kind of captures the spirit of the matter is leech.

There are those who latch onto us to fulfill material or emotional needs that, in all reality, have no business being in our lives to begin with. I'm not talking about mutual relationships where we do things for each other, I'm talking about those who hold one or two things over our heads to psychologically blackmail us into doing their bidding.

Whether it's the boyfriend or girlfriend who demands that we drop everything when they want something, but will not give us the same generosity; or the "friend" who always has a favor to ask, but disappears when we are in need, these people exist through the generosity of kind and good people. These people suck us dry mentally, emotionally, financially and physically, and they're not going to stop because we want them to.

When we surround ourselves with people like this, we are not only enabling a manipulator to continue along with their selfish ways at our expense, we're also not respecting ourselves. It's one thing to be kind, but it's quite another to let someone take and take from us without giving anything in return.

These people have a tendency to always say the right things, but their actions don't match their words. They're masters at deception, and are always looking for their next host.

Sometimes, these people are pity-addicts. That is, people who always have a sob story and gain validation by emotionally sucking kind-hearted people dry. Often times, they'll vehemently refuse any sort of aid or help, but will never stop dragging you under the water with their unfortunate circumstances.

There are a few ways to tell whether someone is a pity-addict, or simply someone that is going through a difficult time. One way is to take a look at their circumstances and the way that they react to them. A pity-addict will usually blame everyone else. Every negative thing that is happening is outside of their control, and they're playing the role of martyr. This person will *always* have at least one thing going wrong, and it's usually the only thing that they'll talk about.

A person who's genuinely going through a difficult time may ask to lean onto you for support, and may break down, but their perspective is much more realistic. If they want help, they will ask for it, but also be doing things to improve things outside of your assistance. If they don't want help, they won't play that game of pushing your assistance away with one hand, while not letting you leave with the other.

In dealing with these sorts of people, use your best judgment. If it's someone who asks a lot of you, but also returns that same consideration when you are in similar need, then there's no issue, and there's no reason to suspect that this person is trying to manipulate you.

If, however, it's someone who requires you to bend over backward, but they are not willing to reciprocate when you are in need, then the best thing that you can do is to end the relationship.

Your peace of mind will thank you.

There are also those who flat out demean,

berate or seek to humiliate and hurt us (physically, emotionally, mentally, sexually, etc.) at every turn. These people act this way to exert power over others and the ultimate goal of these actions is to make you feel inferior, that they're only trying to "correct" you. If this person can make you feel worthless, then they have ultimate power over you. The unfortunate thing is that it's all too common for a person to start believing the abuser.

Many abused people do, or at one point have, blamed themselves for the abuse. "If only I hadn't been home late," or "I burned dinner," etc. The fact is that if you have a person in your life who is doing this to you, it is not your fault, and *they* are the one that has something seriously wrong with them. People like this thrive on killing other people's spirits, and have no right to be in your life. If you find yourself in an abusive relationship and feel like you can't get out on your own, or would just like to talk to someone, call The National Domestic Violence Abuse Hotline at:

1-800-799-7233

or 1-800-787-3224 (TTY)

What about the good people in your life? The ones who make you feel better having spent some time with them? These are the people who accept you for who you are, they are willing to help when they can; they are honest, caring, supportive and loving people who are interested in seeing you achieve *your* dreams, not some notion of what they think you should be.

Not every person who is unhealthy in our lives is abusive, but why should you waste your time with people that don't inspire you? The people who make the most incredible friends are the ones who like you *because* of who you are, not in spite of it. These are the people who will go out of their way to coax a smile out of you when you're having a bad day. Friends like this are worth more than any sum of money a person can possess. It is with such people that we find our happiness enhanced, and our lives enriched.

So, how do you find the good friends and stay away from the bad ones? Well, it's not an immediate thing that you can tell about someone, whether or not they're a genuine person, but if it's someone with whom you have mutual contacts, find out how they treat the people around them. Are they respectful toward new acquaintances and old friends alike? Sometimes, it comes down to simple trial and error. A good friend is someone who is okay with earning your trust, and won't demand it from the get go.

Keep your mind and your eyes open. Everyone makes mistakes, but someone that repeatedly falls short of the trust that you entrust in them isn't likely to change their ways.

For those people in your life who are a positive influence, an inspiration, let them know how much they mean to you. Gratitude is a gift that both parties enjoy

.

CHAPTER 4: BE GOOD TO YOURSELF

Simple enough, right? Well, if that were the case, then it's my suspicion that a lot more people would be doing it.

You might be surprised at how much difference getting proper exercise, being hygienic, organizing your responsibilities and simply standing up for yourself can make.

Let's start with physical health. If we are what we eat, how much of you comes from a fast food franchise? I'm not going to say that eating the occasional hamburger, or indulging in sweets from time to time is bad or even undesirable, however, with the fast-paced world that we've all been convinced that we live in, we often make poor health choices.

"You have to be working all of the time, so here's the energy drink that will keep you productive, the salt, sugar and fat-filled hamburger that'll convince your body that it's being fed long enough for you to make that deadline and here's the newest car (that you should be already be driving; your neighbor down the street has two) to keep you from getting fresh air and exercise!"

It's kind of funny when put that way but, whether it's the intention of these companies or not, they're trying to sell not only a product, but a lifestyle which *requires* that product. The idea that a good product fulfills a need is sort of an anecdote at this point, as through the brilliance of marketing and advertising, it's become simple to create a "need."

But this chapter isn't about wagging a finger at economics; it's about doing what is actually best for you.

The simple fact is that when we eat healthier and we get more exercise, we feel better and are less likely go get sick. Not to mention that these incredibly simple tasks help with our mood and outlook. When we maintain a poor diet and don't get enough exercise, we're more likely to get sick, we feel sluggish and are easily exhausted and are much more likely to suffer not only health problems, but mental problems such as depression and anxiety as well.

When it comes to hygiene, I'm not going to suggest any "beauty tips" or anything like that. The important thing here is to stay clean and well-groomed. When we clean our bodies, the toxins which come through our pores are washed away, and this act can have health benefits outside of the other obvious reasons to stay clean.

Another thing that is all-too-common in our society is allowing ourselves to become so distracted with everything else that we let important things such as bills and other necessities pile up until we're overwhelmed. This can be the cause of a great deal of stress, and it's not uncommon for something to get lost in the shuffle.

One good way to keep track of your bills and other important, time-sensitive papers is to have two small baskets: one for things which need to be taken care of in the first half of the month, and one for things which need to be taken care of in the second half of the month. You can go as far as organizing them into four, weekly receptacles, the point is to organize and prioritize.

When you have a month's worth of bills sitting on the table, even though only some of them need to be taken care of immediately, it's easy to get overwhelmed and to procrastinate doing anything with any of it. By putting such things into an easily acceptable place and breaking them up, you take the pressure off in a way that will keep things together and organized by when they need to be taken care of.

Another great way to take some of the money-worry off of your plate is to create a budget. When you are receiving your bills this next month, write down what your payments are and to where under the heading, "expenses." Along with this, include things such as groceries, parking fees, gas for your vehicle, even entertainment. Try to get as close to accurate an idea of how much is going out every month.

Then, write down your income. Write down whatever you get from wages and/or other sources and place them into a heading called "income." Again, be as thorough as possible. Subtract your expenses from your income and see where you stand financially for the month. If you're well into the black (the positive,) then you can afford to be a bit more lax with the purse-strings, make a larger payment on a debt or save up for a nice vacation. If, however, you're in the red, or you're just scraping by, look over your expenses and see what it is that you can augment in order to achieve better financial stability.

The more information that you give yourself, the better you can plan; not only in making next month's bills, but for the future as well.

Along with eating healthy, getting exercise and managing your finances, another way to de-stress your life and show yourself a little love is to keep a clean home. It's often true that the state of a person's house is often a reflection of a person's mental-state, but this can go both ways.

When we are surrounded by disarray, unwashed dishes, dirty clothes and clutter, it's easy to get bogged down and overwhelmed by the chaos around us. When, however, a home is tidy, there is a sense of well-being that comes with it.

Keeping a clean home shows love to yourself by a physical manifestation of the fact that you need not live in squalor, but deserve a nice home. It doesn't matter if you live in a mansion or a studio apartment, having things cleaned up when possible is one less thing to worry about.

We're going to switch gears here for a moment now, and we're going to talk about how you can be better to yourself in regard to other people. You can do everything else right in the world, but if you allow other people to bully you, pressure you or berate you, you're probably going to find it a lot more difficult to love yourself.

In the previous chapters we discussed a bit about how some people can be negative forces in our lives, but here we're going to focus more on what to do when this sort of thing happens, rather than simple prevention.

Here's a scenario:

Your boss makes you come in late every Friday.

This, in itself, wouldn't bother you so much, except for the fact that you are the only one that he or she ever asks to do this. At first, it seemed as if your boss just had a higher degree for your skills, but then the harassment starts. It begins with a little flirtation, an off-color remark here and there, but now, when everyone else leaves, or in other situations in which the two of you are alone, your boss is frequently making blatant, unwanted advances toward you. You've asked your boss to stop, but he or she hasn't.

What do you do?

The simple and healthy answer is to report this, as it's a clear-cut case of sexual harassment. However, many people are too afraid of retribution, or being made out to be someone looking for attention. It's because of this sort of fear that people like this are still so rampant in the workplace.

If it's making you uncomfortable, and you've asked this person to stop but they haven't, what they're doing isn't only hurtful, it's illegal.

In this case, the best way that you can stand up for yourself is to report your boss to his superior, HR and/or the police. In this case, you're not only standing up for yourself, you're standing up for every other person that your boss would harass in the future.

Another scenario:

When you're out with your friends, you usually have a really good time, but one of the members of your circle has an affinity for putting you down.

Every time that you share an accomplishment, or a new, exciting prospect, this person is quick to dismiss what you're saying in a rude and unceremonious fashion.

Your friends kind of shrug it off, but it's really starting to get on your nerves how this person likes to make you appear weaker and less successful than they are. They often flat out call you stupid or some other demeaning term, just to make him or herself seem a bit more powerful. So, do you say something, possibly making your friends uncomfortable, or do you just grin and bear it to avoid rocking the boat? There is a third option here, but we'll get to it in a moment.

While a person is entitled to their opinion, no matter how asinine it may be, that doesn't mean that a person has the right to publicly or privately berate or try to humiliate you.

The thing that, for some, makes this sort of situation more complex is that the offender is a part of the main social group, and therefore, cutting this person out of their life seems like it would cause more damage than it would repair.

The fact of the matter is that nobody deserves to be talked to and treated that way. If nobody else is going to step in and put an end to it, for your own self-esteem and self-love, you need to. Maybe your friends were too uncomfortable to say something, or they didn't realize that you were being hurt, but that leads us to the third option.

If someone is demeaning you in front of your friends and they're not doing anything about it when it's clearly not a joke, it's not playful banter, it's nothing but hurtful, are they the kind of people that you really need as friends? You already know that they're not going to stand up for you. What if the situation was worse? How much farther would they be from your aid?

In my opinion, the best thing to do in this situation would be to first, let the person know that you don't appreciate the junk that they say to you and let them know that you're not going to tolerate it; and next to tell your friends that if they're unwilling to stand up for you when someone is hurting you that they're not the kind of people that you want in your life. Sometimes people will hear the wakeup call and change their ways, but I wouldn't let them back in without making them earn some trust back.

There are countless possible scenarios, and many different approaches, but by standing up for yourself, you are empowered. You *show* yourself love by not allowing others to trample all over you. You prove to yourself that you are worthy of being treated with the same respect with which you treat others... and you might even inspire someone else to stand up for themselves when they're being treated wrongly.

CHAPTER 5: OF BALANCE AND GENEROSITY

In this chapter, we will be covering two of the most important things that you can do to show yourself love: generosity and balance. We will begin with balance, as it is the more delicate of these two procedures.

By balance is meant taking the time for all of the areas of your life. Some people have a tendency to work to the exclusion of other things, for others, work is the farthest thing from their mind. There are so many things in our lives that it can often seem impossible to do the balancing act, however, the consequences of imbalance far outweigh the hassle of gaining equilibrium.

So, how can we go about finding this balance in

our lives? First of all, it's important to investigate the way in which you actually spend your time. Off the top of your head, it's easy to say, "Well, I work from nine-to-five, then I come home." While this may be true, it's not the whole story. When you're at work, could you use some more discipline, or could you stand to relax a little bit? When you come home, where does your focus go? Does it go to family, friends, television; internet?

None of these things are bad in-and-of themselves, in fact, each can serve a healthy, useful function in our lives. It's when this equilibrium is skewed too far in one direction that we find other necessary aspects of our lives wanting.

How much time do you spend working, whether at the office or at home? How does this compare to the time that you spend in social pursuits, whether with family or friends? How much, if any, time do you spend alone, just taking some time for yourself? These are all very important areas in our lives, and when we neglect one, we tend to be less happy, more stressed and more overwhelmed by the proposition of doing anything else.

So show yourself some love by taking some

time to reflect on how you spend an average day; an average week. When you're home, is work still the pervasive force in your mind? When you're at work, are you daydreaming and inattentive? What about your social life? Do you spend enough time with friends and family? Too much?

There's no magical ratio here, what works for one may work for another, but when there's a serious imbalance in your life, it does show not only to others, but to your inner-self.

A balanced life is a happy life is a life of loving yourself. We all have needs, and no matter how big that paycheck is, it's not going to make you happy if you're missing out on the life that you've always wanted to live. At the same time, sitting at home alone, drinking beer and watching television isn't going to go far in meeting all of your needs either.

What is it that you're missing out on? What would you do if only there were more hours in the day, and what will it take for you to realize that the answer to that question is indicative of a need that's not being met.

There are other aspects to our lives than work, rest, social experience and alone-time, but these are certainly at the top of the list. To these four aspects, add in the things which are of particular importance to you. Is there a hobby that you enjoy, but can never quite find the time for? Do you enjoy giving back to your community, but always seem to be too busy to make it there? Find what is holding you back, and from there, you can make the effort to bring a balance which is appropriate to your needs into your life.

Last, but certainly not least, is generosity, both to yourself and to others, because truly being generous to others is kindness to yourself.

We can't all be millionaire philanthropists, but there are things that we can do in our own lives to show generosity to others. We don't even have to look outside of our families, our friends or our co-workers to find an opportunity to give a little time, effort or money to help someone in need, or just do something nice for someone who could use it.

One of the most self-affirming things that a person can do is to be generous. It's not necessary to bankrupt yourself, or even to necessarily spend a dime to provide generosity to another. When we are generous, we are showing to ourselves more than anyone else that we are worthy and capable of love. True love, whether it's self-love or love between two or more people, doesn't require that we hold onto it and keep it to ourselves. In fact, true love wants to be shared, and thrives on giving.

It is also important to be generous with *yourself*.

Realize that your feelings are valid. Reward yourself when you have made an achievement in your life. Most of all, realize that we all make mistakes and it's what we do after the fact that makes all of the difference.

When we learn from our mistakes and the mistakes of others, we are showing generosity toward our inner-selves by showing ourselves that we're not going to put ourselves through whatever the needless turmoil was any more. Sometimes it takes a mistake to learn a lesson, what really matters is that we learn that lesson and move on.

When you're out on the town or having a conversation comes up, don't be afraid to share your accomplishments. Granted, there's a difference between showing pride in what you do and being an arrogant blowhard, but I think that's a difference that we can all understand. If the context fits, throw in an anecdote about something you're proud of.

What it really comes down to is not being overly critical of your emotions, even when you know that they're misplaced. It's more important to understand why you're feeling the way that you're feeling, positive or negative, than it is to scold or belittle yourself for it. All that the latter does is to make things worse and gets in the way of loving ourselves.

Learn to trust your instincts, for instinct, tempered by experience and an open-mind will seldom lead you astray. Forging a stronger relationship with your loved ones or your higher power, should you believe in one, will only help to reinforce your own ideals, your beliefs and your values, and it is from these that all else issues forth.

In a way, every suggestion in this book has a connection with being generous to yourself. Generosity is, after all, a large part of what love is.

Show others that you're worthy of being respected and loved by being respectful and loving, and by standing up for yourself when someone tries to come along and knock you down. The first and most important ally that you have in the world is yourself. You deserve to be loved.

CHAPTER 6: WHO YOU ARE

Oftentimes the catalyst for change lies within a few simple words. Why? Because they remind us of who we are; something that can be very easy to forget. Whether it's "I love you" or "I believe in you" the force behind these beautifully woven letters has the power to affect us in the most profound ways. As this book draws to a close, I would like to leave you with a few words to inspire you along your journey to self-love.

As you softly speak the following phrases to yourself, let them always be a reminder to you of the respect, love and value that *every* life is worthy of receiving.

I am one in a billion.

You may feel the pull of your imperfections

from time to time but know that the only person, who can ever go the furthest in your life, is you. You are one in a billion and your life is a unique story that only you have the voice to tell. Attaining inner peace isn't about letting someone else read your lines; it's about embracing your character and giving the performance of a lifetime. Never be afraid to express your inner thoughts, never be afraid to dance to a different beat because when you shine with self-acceptance, you light up the world.

I appreciate myself.

I acknowledge and celebrate the wonderful things about me. Begin by making a conscious effort to express gratitude towards yourself for a job well done. Too often low self-esteem leads us to down play our role in success by giving all the credit to someone else. While it is important to show appreciation to all members involved for a job well done, it is imperative to take a moment to acknowledge your contribution to the achievement. By recognizing the value in yourself, you set the expectation for others to do the same.

I am accepting.

Because I love and accept myself, I am more

accepting of others. We can only restore our self-esteem and feel good about ourselves if we accept ourselves as we are. Each person is wholly unique and each comes with his or her own unique strengths and weaknesses. Accepting both the strengths and weaknesses gives us the humility we ultimately need to forge a true bond with our fellows as well as the boost we need to feel good about ourselves. In doing so, we create a healthy and positive self-esteem.

I am powerful.

While you may not be able to control the circumstance, you determine how you will allow it to define you. Never fall into feelings of despair, for within you is the power to see the wisdom in every event and allow it to make you stronger. When you make a mistake or things don't go according to plan, resist the urge to blame yourself. Instead, mentally step back and look for the lesson unfolding before you. Without weakness there would never be strength and each time you allow yourself to see the wisdom in the challenge, you give your chance to emerge a stronger, more confident person.

I am adventurous.

I speak up, I try new recipes, I go on first dates. I am not afraid to step outside of my cozy comfort zone. Whether it's trying out a new dish at your favorite restaurant, creating a savings plan or buying a one-way ticket, take one step today that will bring you closer to your dreams. In doing so, you make your vision real and it's no longer just a thought floating around in your head. It suddenly transforms into tangible goal that you are actively working to bring about.

I have my own mind.

I define myself based on my own thoughts and opinions and not those of others. Like pinpoints on a map, choices create a mental path that can lead you towards or away from your dreams. Each choice that you make to be happy, each choice that you make to never be defeated and every choice that you make to push on will aid you in manifesting what you truly desire in your life. Just as gas fuels a car, the choices that you make fuel you on the journey to reaching your goals.

I am in alignment.

I did not get these scars by accepting someone else's ideal and I will never stop fighting for myself. When you are able to gauge what is important to you in life, the next step is to look at your life and determine if you are aligned with your principles. Whatever it is that drives you, ensure you incorporate it into your life each and every day. Is giving to others your passion? Then give out smiles to those you meet along the way. Does the thought of success get you out of bed in the morning? If so, always remember to congratulate yourself on your achievements throughout the day, no matter how small the task. Are you a lover of nature? Get out of the office and walk to a green space on your lunch break.

I am faith in action.

I don't have all the solutions but I am not afraid to try and go for my dreams. Like a sailboat we move with the wind of our beliefs. When our beliefs are weak it's difficult to move our boat forward and we are only able to drift on the current and pray that it leads us to a safe harbor. However, when our belief is strong enough to fill our sails we move forward full speed in that direction. The important thing to remember is that beliefs do not discriminate so if you are fueling your sail with negative beliefs, nine times out of ten you will not have a positive outcome. When you fill your sails with positive beliefs it propels you forward in the right direction.

I am love.

You are worthy of love, you are worthy of respect and though you may not always find love in someone else, make certain that you always find it within yourself. By encouraging yourself and not beating yourself down, you open yourself up to receiving even more love.

As you journey through life, remember to always take the bad times along with the good and never let them conquer you because no bond is stronger than that of love. Love has the power to heal all wounds and with each passing day may the loving bond that you forge within yourself, strengthen you always.

CONCLUSION

Loving one's self is not the same thing as conceit. Love is kind, it's thoughtful and it's ever growing, ever changing; while conceit is only a form of deception, akin to a blowfish puffing itself up because of its fear of natural predators.

There is no more worthwhile pursuit in the world than to love and to be loved. It's not always easy to see it in the world today, but there is more love than can ever be expressed, and it all starts within you. Each and every one of us is a source of love, and that in-and-of itself is a pretty spectacular thing.

When we love ourselves, we are more capable of loving other people. Our self-worth goes up, we're happier, healthier and we take better care of ourselves and of those around us. I hope that in these pages, you have found some insight and some workable things that you can do in your own life to show yourself a little more love.

When we don't love ourselves, it becomes impossible to feel love from others, no matter how present it may be. There's always that nagging, fallacious statement, "I'm unworthy of love." The fact of the matter is that this is simply untrue. When we give up on ourselves, that's when things really start to go badly. If more people loved themselves, there wouldn't be so much senseless conflict in the world. If more people could find trust and generosity within themselves, we might finally all be able to push past our differences and come together as people on this planet.

It all starts with you.

Love is trusting and worthy of trust. When we learn to trust our instincts, learn from and forgive ourselves for our own mistakes, understand our feelings and stick up for ourselves, we create a much brighter world in which to grow and experience this crazy thing called life.

With that, I wish you all of the love in the world.

Preview of "The Seeds of Beauty: Defining Your Beauty & Style from the Inside Out"

The Burning Ship

"The virtue lies in the struggle, not the prize."

Richard Monckton Milnes, *The World to the Soul*

On the journey to becoming our better selves, there is always a risk. In essence we are leaving behind the only way we have ever known, however self-destructive it may be. The best analogy I could use here is a burning ship.

Negative thoughts have a way of gaining momentum like a fire stoked by a fiercely moving wind until they quickly surround us with smoke so thick it is hard for us to see through the haze. No matter how much others love us, how many admire us, or how successful our lives may be, we find it harder and harder to breathe.

Trapped on the burning ship that is our inner self, the only way to escape the engulfment is to jump into the water waiting below. The choice to jump can stem from a variety of reasons. It could be a life-changing illness, a divorce from an unhappy marriage, or simply waking up to the fact that we want more for ourselves. Tentatively, we cross the deck and are ready to take the leap. Then, screaming from the abyss of our souls, we take the leap off the ship and land safely into the cool, refreshing waters.

Relieved, we feel the intense sensation of a new start, a new beginning. Happily we laugh as ripples of freedom break through the surface of the water with our every movement. And then the inevitable happens.

We look to the shore and suddenly realize how far away it is. Can we swim that far?

Panic sets in.

We look back at the burning ship and begin to desperately rationalize. Maybe if we splash water on the deck, the flames will retreat and it won't be so bad. Sure, the boat isn't in the best condition, but maybe, just maybe, despite all the holes, it will still make it to shore.

Change can bring a sense of vulnerability to anyone experiencing it. It can be very frightening to step out into new waters. Instinctively, we retreat to what makes us feel safe and secure even if it's a burning ship. Then without realizing it we, like the burning ship, sink back into the same negative patterns of the past. We try to reassure ourselves that it wouldn't have worked out anyway, but in truth we never know because we were too scared to venture beyond our fear.

As you work to better yourself both internally and externally, you may feel the fear that often accompanies change. Like many before you, you will see the distance to the shore and look back to the burning ship. This is a natural reaction that does not indicate weakness.

But instead of returning, you have to make the conscious decision to swim away from the burning ship. With each stroke you will fight the currents of doubt, and each kick will strengthen you and propel you toward your goal. You will tire as everyone inevitably does. But instead of letting yourself sink into the depths of naysayers, float on your back and rest for a bit. Let the waves of hope and the belief in yourself carry you toward shore. And when you are rested and feel strong again, roll over and start to swim again, and don't stop the journey until you reach the shore.

There have been many burning ships in my life

from which I have been forced to jump—bad relationships, dead-end jobs, and self-destructive behavior, to name an attractive few.

And because I have the tendency to be stubborn, I have experienced the pain of repeat voyages. How did I learn to stop setting my ships on fire? I began to look for the warning signs. There is always smoke before the flames. When you smell the smoke, which can appear in the form of self-destructive thoughts, insecurities, or pressures to conform to someone else's ideals, stop what you are doing and look to see where the smoke is coming from.

Is this self-induced? Are the people with whom you associate healthy for your well-being? Has someone in the past told you that you weren't good enough, and though buried in the years of your past, the heat of it still burns subconsciously?

If you follow the smoke, you will find the source of your fire. And once you locate it, you possess the ability to squelch it before it turns into a rampant blaze. In doing so you will not only gain insight about yourself, you will also strengthen yourself for the future.

When faced with a hardship in life, it is not

uncommon to feel surrounded and entrapped with the emotions of fear, anger, and doubt. However, the next time you feel the four walls around you beginning to inch themselves inward, mentally stand on your tiptoes and peek over the top of the wall to look beyond your current state.

Time keeps moving forward and so will you, even if it's only one small step at a time.

Beauty Brainstorm:

> Without judgment, pause and take a moment to acknowledge any burning ships that are in your life. Write about each one.

> Mentally tracing back the smoke, what was it in your life that initiated the blaze?

> What fears have returned you to the burning ship? Looking back at my voyages, the fear of loneliness as well as unmet expectations contributed to repeat journeys. What are yours?

> In your journal, describe what you have learned as a result of the hardship. Look for the lesson in everything and remember to keep your focus forward.

Bridging the Gap

"To love is human, it is also human to forgive."

Plautus, *Mercator*

In the last chapter, you identified the smoke that aided in the creation of previous fires. The smoke has led you to the initial flames, now what?

What steps do you take to extinguish them?

Start by addressing the source of your fires with forgiveness and acceptance. The past is exactly that—the past. Now is the time, at the beginning of your journey, to have a heart-to-heart with yourself. Address each wisp of smoke with attention and care, as you would with a friend. If you have pent-up feelings or unvoiced thoughts, clear the smoke in the air by writing out those unspoken words or speaking them aloud—even if it's only quietly to yourself. We look so often to others for validation and closure, when in reality true acceptance begins with ourselves.

Let each word fall from your thoughts like

droplets of water over the flames until the fire is gently put out. Then mentally open the windows until the smoke begins to clear. With each subtle breeze, feel the negative energy exiting your core and leaving a quiet space for you to reconnect with yourself.

Every time a self-destructive thought enters your head, drawing from the power within you, send a mental love note to yourself to say, "I love you and I accept you as you are." Each time you address a negative thought with love, you weaken its power and in turn positively contribute to your self-esteem.

Fires are destructive in that they have the power to lay waste to even the strongest of structures, leaving behind confusion and feelings of pain. However, each fire also leaves behind a rich soil full of minerals and nutrients that allow us to grow back stronger. In this soil, plant your seeds of beauty and lovingly watch them grow. You will soon find that makeup and beautiful new clothes are no longer tools to cover what you don't like about yourself. They will now be tools to enhance the beauty that is truly your own.

Now is the time for you to make the commitment to evolve into a stronger, more compassionate and beautiful you.

Not ten pounds from now. Not ten years from now. *Right now.*

Since my early years, I have been taught the importance of forgiveness. The message was as constant as a quiet stream flowing through my life and as essential as breathing. Forgiveness came grudgingly at first, usually following my siblings either taking or breaking my toys. Yet despite the crashing waves of anger that I felt, there was something of a relief in knowing I didn't have to carry around the burden of anger with someone I loved. However, as good as it felt to forgive another, I think the turning point for me came when I learned to forgive myself.

Admittedly, it has been one of the scariest things that I have had to do in my life. It was almost as if it were essential for me to remind myself of missteps in order to make sure they didn't happen again. Could I be trusted not to let myself down in future?

What I failed to realize is that while I had successfully built an emotional nest to seemingly protect myself, the only thing I truly accomplished was clipping my own wings. How can you expect to fly when you are weighted down with chains that hold yourself and your heart to the past?

Have you ever tried to pick up an item when your hands are full? Nine times out of ten you've had to set something down so that your hands were free to take hold of what you wanted to grasp.

Sometimes your heart, like your hands, is filled with thoughts of the past and worries of the future that make it difficult to move forward in the present.

In order to embrace what you truly want in life, it's important to release your grip on the past in order to free up space in your heart.

Here is an affirmation of inner beauty to remind you of the relationship that we must continually build and develop no matter what our stage in life.

Speak the following affirmation of inner beauty aloud until its true meaning resonates within you.

Commitment to Beauty Affirmation

[Your name],

To you, I will never be a fair-weather friend.

When you are afraid,

I will give you the courage to step forward.

If ever you make a mistake,

I will never lose faith in you.

And when you begin to doubt how

beautiful you are, I will remind you.

Today and every day

I promise to always stand by you.

You are me. I am you.

I love you.

Beauty Brainstorm:

Print out this beauty affirmation from http://www.theseedsofbeauty.com and carry it with you for the next thirty days. Pull it out and let it serve as a reminder of how beautiful, resilient, and human you are.

What wisps of smoke need your loving attention? What words have you been longing to say? Quietly speak or write these weighted words here.

Letting go begins with not only accepting circumstances, but also accepting your emotions. Instead of burying your feelings, acknowledge that you are upset, acknowledge that you are angry, and acknowledge that you are human. By releasing these emotions, you free up space to heal.

Get to the heart of the matter and ask yourself, "Why am I holding on to this?" Write down your insights in your journal. By understanding an underlying issue, you can begin to take corrective action.

Never underestimate the power of forgiveness. Through forgiveness you let go of your burden and find strength in the wisdom that has taken its place. #

EXPLORE MORE FROM THIS AUTHOR

Below you'll find some of my other books that are popular on Amazon and Kindle as well. Alternatively, you can visit my author page on Amazon to see other work done by me.

The Seeds of Beauty: Defining Your Beauty & Style From the Inside Out

Write to Make it Right: How Journaling Can Lead to a Happier, More Fulfilled Life

The Glass Half Full: How to Be Positive & Why it's Healthy for You

Sorry is The Hardest Word - A Guide to Apologizing & How to Do It

Subscribe My Free Newsletter.
When you sign up to receive my newsletter, you'll periodically receive *powerful* life lessons and inspirational insights to reach your goals, stay motivated and be your personal best. To subscribe, type this URL into your favorite browser to sign up: http://bit.ly/1rusEGd

ABOUT THE AUTHOR

 Author Lakeysha-Marie Green is no stranger to tackling style dilemmas. A fashion stylist and former women's fit technologist, her extensive experience in the fashion industry taught her the importance of fit, fashion, and effortless style.

Her penchant for creativity led to her work in editorial magazines, international film premieres, and advertising. Inspired by her own roller coaster ride to self-discovery, Lakeysha-Marie began writing to illustrate the beautiful potential for transformation that lies within us all. Her first book, *The Seeds of Beauty*, tells an inspiring story of restoring unconditional self-love and genuinely radiating your beauty from within.

Lakeysha-Marie holds a degree in Fashion Design & Merchandising, with continued coursework in Styling & Photography from the London College of Fashion.

ONE LAST THING...

If you believe the book is worth sharing, please would you take a few seconds to let others on Amazon know about it? If it turns out to make a difference in their lives, they'll be forever grateful to you, as will I.

All the best,

Lakeysha-Marie